Math Masters

Operations and Algebraic Thinking

THE HISTORY OF NEW YORK CITY

Understand Properties of Multiplication

Katie White

PowerKiDS
press™

NEW YORK

Published in 2015 by The Rosen Publishing Group, Inc.
29 East 21st Street, New York, NY 10010

Book Design: Jonathan J. D'Rozario

Photo Credits: Cover, p. 9 IM _Photo/Shutterstock.com; pp. 3, 4, 6, 8, 10, 12, 14, 16, 18, 20, 22, 23, 24 (statue) John T
Takai/Shutterstock.com; pp. 3, 4, 6, 8, 10, 12, 14, 16, 18, 20, 22, 23, 24 (background) Nik Merkulov/Shutterstock.com; p. 5
(map) Rainer Lesniewski/Shutterstock.com; p. 5 (main) Songquan Deng/Shutterstock.com; p. 7 Rudi Von Briel/Stockbyte/
Getty Images; p. 11 T photography/Shutterstock.com; p. 13 ChameleonsEye/Shutterstock.com; p. 15 Frank11/Shutterstock.
com; p. 17 (main) a katz/Shutterstock.com; p. 17 (ball) http://en.wikipedia.org/wiki/File:Times_Square_New_Year%27s_
Eve_Ball_2009.jpg#file; p. 19 Mihai Andritoiu/Shutterstock.com; p. 21 ValeStock/Shutterstock.com; p. 22 Erika Cross/
Shutterstock.com.

Library of Congress Cataloging-in-Publication Data
White, Katie, 1977-
The history of New York City : understand properties of multiplication / Katie White.

        pages cm. — (Math masters. Operations and algebraic thinking)

 Includes index.
ISBN 978-1-4777-4958-6 (pbk.)
ISBN 978-1-4777-4957-9 (6-pack)
ISBN 978-1-4777-6449-7 (library binding)
1. Multiplication—Juvenile literature. 2. New York (N.Y.)—Juvenile literature. I. Title.
QA115.W57 2015
513.2′13—dc23
                                2014002188

Manufactured in the United States of America

CPSIA Compliance Information: Batch #WS15RC: For further information contact Rosen Publishing, New York, New York at 1-800-237-9932.

Contents

A Special City

Have you ever been to New York City? You've probably seen it in movies or on television. It's one of the most important cities in the world.

New York City has the highest population of any U.S. city—over 8 million people! It's home to people of many different **cultures**, or ways of life. New York City has 5 parts, called boroughs: Manhattan, Brooklyn, Queens, Staten Island, and the Bronx.

New York City has a very interesting history. For a short time in the late 1700s, it was the capital of the United States!

New York City

THE BRONX

NEW YORK

NEW JERSEY

East River

Hudson River

MANHATTAN

QUEENS

BROOKLYN

STATEN ISLAND

ATLANTIC OCEAN

The Erie Canal

New York City became important by being in a good place for trade. Because it's on the coast, it was easy for ships to reach. Also, in 1825, the Erie Canal was finished. This man-made waterway connected New York City to inland cities.

The Erie Canal connects the Hudson River to Lake Erie near Buffalo, New York. The Hudson River connects the canal to New York City. The Erie Canal made New York City the busiest port in America!

Many **barges** traveled on the Erie Canal. If you saw 5 groups with 3 barges each on the canal, you saw 15 barges altogether. You can multiply these factors in any order. The product, or the answer, is always 15.

$5 \times 3 = 15$
$3 \times 5 = 15$

Central Park

Central Park was built in the middle of Manhattan between 1858 and 1873. Before the park was built, people in the city had nowhere to go to escape crowded neighborhoods. Frederick Law Olmsted created the idea for the park. It included 36 bridges, 6 bodies of water, and plenty of grassy space.

Today, Central Park covers 843 acres (341 ha) of land. It's filled with fountains, monuments, and artwork.

Many people take rowboats out on the water in Central Park. If you see 6 boats, each with 3 people, you see 18 people altogether. 6 times 3 is the same as 3 times 6. You can use division to check your answer.

$6 \times 3 = 18$
$3 \times 6 = 18$

check your answer ⟶

$18 \div 3 = 6$
$18 \div 6 = 3$

The Brooklyn Bridge

The New York City skyline is one of the most well-known sights in the world. A skyline is a view of buildings against the sky. Pictures of the New York City skyline often include the Brooklyn Bridge.

This bridge, finished in 1883, connects Manhattan and Brooklyn. Building the bridge took 14 years and 600 workers! It's a suspension bridge, which means it's held up by cables that pass over towers. About 150,000 people use this bridge every day.

In 1884, 21 elephants walked across the Brooklyn Bridge. Imagine 7 rows of 3 elephants. That makes 21. It's the same total number as 3 rows of 7 elephants.

7 x 3 = 21
3 x 7 = 21

Brooklyn Bridge

Ellis Island

The reason New York City is home to so many cultures is because it was the first stop for many immigrants coming to the United States. Immigrants are people who come from one country to live in another. Many immigrants came here for freedom and a new beginning.

Ellis Island was a huge immigration station, which opened in 1892. It was the first place that 12 million immigrants saw as they arrived in America.

Imagine you're at Ellis Island in 1892. You see 3 groups of 2 people enter a gate 5 times. When you have more than 2 numbers to multiply, you need to multiply 2 numbers at a time. For example, with the equation $3 \times 2 \times 5$, you can multiply 3 and 2 to get 6. Then, you can multiply 6 and 5. That's 30 people altogether.

$$(3 \times 2) \times 5 = 30$$
$$6 \times 5 = 30$$

Ellis Island

Times Square

Some people know New York City as the "city that never sleeps" because of its bright lights and nighttime activities. Perhaps the best example of this side of New York City is Times Square.

Times Square was named for the *New York Times* when the newspaper moved there in 1904. Today, it's one of the most visited places in the world. It has huge screens that show **advertisements**. There are giant stores and **restaurants**, too.

Imagine you see 5 groups of 5 signs 2 times. To find the total number, you can multiply 5 times 5 to get 25. Then multiply 25 times 2 to get 50. There's another way to find the answer.

(5 x 5) x 2 = 50
25 x 2 = 50

or

(2 x 5) x 5 = 50
10 x 5 = 50

How do you like to spend your New Year's Eve? Many New Yorkers and visitors from all over the world spend it in Times Square for the yearly ball drop. That's when a giant, light-covered ball is lowered at midnight.

The first New Year's ball drop happened in 1907. The first ball, covered in 100 lightbulbs, was 5 feet (1.5 m) tall! The ball has been replaced many times. Each new ball shines brighter than the last!

Imagine you count 4 groups of 5 lightbulbs 5 times. You can multiply 4 times 5 to get 20, and then multiply 20 times 5 to get 100. Can you think of another way to find the answer?

$$(4 \times 5) \times 5 = 100$$
$$20 \times 5 = 100$$

Times Square ball

All Aboard!

Grand Central Terminal is the largest train station in the world and an important New York City building. It's a railroad terminal, or place where trains stop. It opened in 1913 at a time when railroads were the best way to travel.

The **ceiling** was painted to look like the night sky. Imagine you count 7 groups with 8 stars each on the ceiling. Multiplying 7 times 8 can be hard, so you can break down the equation to be easier.

To break down the equation, keep one of the numbers—7. Split the number 8 into 2 smaller numbers, such as 5 and 3. Then, you make 2 multiplication equations with the smaller numbers. The answer to 7 times 5 is 35, and the answer to 7 times 3 is 21. Last, add 35 and 21 together to get 56.

$$7 \times 8 = ?$$
$$(7 \times 5) + (7 \times 3) = ?$$
$$35 + 21 = 56$$

A Reader's Dream!

The New York Public Library is every reader's dream. It's a public library system that's made up of 87 branches. The branches have about 53 million items, including books, CDs, magazines, and maps.

The New York Public Library was established in 1849, but the main building wasn't built until 1911. It's located on Fifth Avenue. Imagine you count 4 groups of 12 books on a shelf at the library. How many do you count altogether?

You can break down this equation. Keep the number 4. Then break 12 down into 10 and 2. Your new equation would be: $(4 \times 10) + (4 \times 2)$. The answer to 4 times 10 is 40, and the answer to 4 times 2 is 8. Add 40 and 8 together to get 48!

$$4 \times 12 = ?$$
$$(4 \times 10) + (4 \times 2) = ?$$
$$40 + 8 = 48$$

21

What's in Your City?

New York City is a special place. It's full of important buildings, parks, and museums. There are many places where you can go to see art, dance, movies, and plays. Each place has its own interesting history.

Next time you're walking around your own city, try to really look at the buildings around you. It can be fun to find out their stories!

The Museum of Modern Art, also called MoMA, is a great place to visit in New York City! Opened in 1929, it's home to some of the most important new artwork in the world.

Glossary

advertisement (ad-vuhr-TYZ-muhnt) Something that tells people about things to buy or things that are happening.

barge (BAHRJ) A long, large boat with a flat bottom for carrying goods.

ceiling (SEE-lihng) The overhead surface of a room.

culture (KUHL-chur) The language, customs, ideas, and art of a group of people.

restaurant (REHS-tuh-rahnt) A place where you can buy and eat meals.

Index

Due to the changing nature of Internet links, The Rosen Publishing Group, Inc., has developed an online list of websites related to the subject of this book. This site is updated regularly. Please use this link to access the list: www.powerkidslinks.com/mm/oat/hnyc